Francis Frith's
Poole & Sandbanks

LEIGH HATTS was born in Bournemouth and grew up familiar with neighbouring Poole. He studied the history of Sandbanks and Poole's coast when pioneering the Bournemouth Coast Path which has extended the Dorset Coast Path beyond Poole Bay. His godfather was the artist Leslie Ward, whose drawings of the quay can be seen in the Waterfront Museum.

MARION MARPLES was born in Poole. She attended Parkstone Grammar School and when a teenager she completed the Poole Harbour swim. As Secretary of the Confraternity of St James, which promotes interest in pilgrimage to Santiago de Compostela in Spain, she has researched Poole's important role as a pilgrim port recorded by the scallop shells on the town's arms.

Photographic Memories

Francis Frith's
Poole & Sandbanks

Leigh Hatts & Marion Marples

First published in the United Kingdom in 2001 by
The Francis Frith Collection

Hardback Edition 2001
ISBN 1-85937-416-6

Paperback Edition 2001
ISBN 1-85937-251-1

Reprinted in Paperback 2002, 2005

British Library Cataloguing in Publication Data

Francis Frith's Poole & Sandbanks
Leigh Hatts & Marion Marples
ISBN 1-85937-251-1

The Francis Frith Collection
Frith's Barn, Teffont,
Salisbury, Wiltshire SP3 5QP
Tel: +44 (0) 1722 716 376
Email: info@francisfrith.co.uk
www.francisfrith.co.uk

Printed and bound in Great Britain

Front Cover: The Custom House 1904 52814t

The colour-tinting is for illustrative purposes only, and is not intended to be historically accurate

AS WITH ANY HISTORICAL DATABASE THE FRITH ARCHIVE IS CONSTANTLY BEING CORRECTED AND IMPROVED
AND THE PUBLISHERS WOULD WELCOME INFORMATION ON OMISSIONS OR INACCURACIES

Contents

Francis Frith: *Victorian Pioneer*

FRANCIS FRITH, Victorian founder of the world-famous photographic archive, was a complex and multi-talented man. A devout Quaker and a highly successful Victorian businessman, he was both philosophical by nature and pioneering in outlook.

By 1855 Francis Frith had already established a wholesale grocery business in Liverpool, and sold it for the astonishing sum of £200,000, which is the equivalent today of over £15,000,000. Now a very rich man, he was able to indulge his passion for travel. As a child he had pored over travel books written by early explorers, and his fancy and imagination had been stirred by family holidays to the sublime mountain regions of Wales and Scotland. 'What lands of spirit-stirring and enriching scenes and places!' he had written. He was to return to these scenes of grandeur in later years to 'recapture the thousands of vivid and tender memories', but with a different purpose. Now in his thirties, and captivated by the new science of photography, Frith set out on a series of pioneering journeys to the Nile regions that occupied him from 1856 until 1860.

Intrigue and Adventure

He took with him on his travels a specially-designed wicker carriage that acted as both dark-room and sleeping chamber. These far-flung journeys were packed with intrigue and adventure. In his life story, written when he was sixty-three, Frith tells of being held captive by bandits, and of fighting 'an awful midnight battle to the very point of surrender with a deadly pack of hungry, wild dogs'. Sporting flowing Arab costume, Frith arrived at Akaba by camel sixty years before Lawrence, where he encountered 'desert princes and rival sheikhs, blazing with jewel-hilted swords'.

During these extraordinary adventures he was assiduously exploring the desert regions bordering the Nile and patiently recording the antiquities and peoples with his camera. He was the first photographer to venture beyond the sixth cataract. Africa was still the mysterious 'Dark Continent', and Stanley and Livingstone's historic meeting was a decade into the future. The conditions for picture taking confound belief. He laboured for hours in his wicker dark-room in the sweltering heat of the desert, while the volatile chemicals fizzed dangerously in their trays. Often he was forced to work in remote tombs and caves where conditions were cooler. Back in London he exhibited his photographs and was 'rapturously cheered' by members of the Royal Society. His reputation as a

photographer was made overnight. An eminent modern historian has likened their impact on the population of the time to that on our own generation of the first photographs taken on the surface of the moon.

Venture of a Life-Time

Characteristically, Frith quickly spotted the opportunity to create a new business as a specialist publisher of photographs. He lived in an era of immense and sometimes violent change. For the poor in the early part of Victoria's reign work was a drudge and the hours long, and people had precious little free time to enjoy themselves. Most had no transport other than a cart or gig at their disposal, and had not travelled far beyond the boundaries of their own town or village. However,

by the 1870s, the railways had threaded their way across the country, and Bank Holidays and half-day Saturdays had been made obligatory by Act of Parliament. All of a sudden the ordinary working man and his family were able to enjoy days out and see a little more of the world.

With characteristic business acumen, Francis Frith foresaw that these new tourists would enjoy having souvenirs to commemorate their days out. In 1860 he married Mary Ann Rosling and set out with the intention of photographing every city, town and village in Britain. For the next thirty years he travelled the country by train and by pony and trap, producing fine photographs of seaside resorts and beauty spots that were keenly bought by millions of Victorians. These prints were painstakingly pasted into family albums and pored over during the dark nights of winter, rekindling precious memories of summer excursions.

The Rise of Frith & Co

Frith's studio was soon supplying retail shops all over the country. To meet the demand he gathered about him a small team of photographers, and published the work of independent artist-photographers of the calibre of Roger Fenton and Francis Bedford. In order to gain some understanding of the scale of Frith's business one only has to look at the catalogue issued by Frith & Co in 1886: it runs to some 670 pages, listing not only many thousands of views of the British Isles but also many photographs of most European countries, and China, Japan, the USA and Canada — note the sample page shown on page 9 from the hand-written *Frith & Co* ledgers detailing pictures taken. By 1890 Frith had created the greatest specialist photographic publishing company in the world,

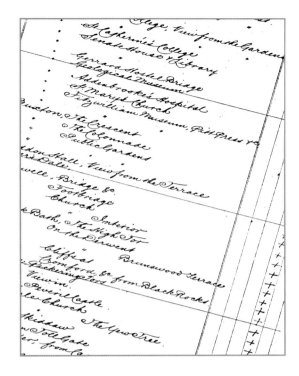

with over 2,000 outlets – more than the combined number that Boots and WH Smith have today! The picture on the right shows the *Frith & Co* display board at Ingleton in the Yorkshire Dales (left of window). Beautifully constructed with a mahogany frame and gilt inserts, it could display up to a dozen local scenes.

Postcard Bonanza

The ever-popular holiday postcard we know today took many years to develop. In 1870 the Post Office issued the first plain cards, with a pre-printed stamp on one face. In 1894 they allowed other publishers' cards to be sent through the mail with an attached adhesive halfpenny stamp. Demand grew rapidly, and in 1895 a new size of postcard was permitted called the court card, but there was little room for illustration. In 1899, a year after

Frith's death, a new card measuring 5.5 x 3.5 inches became the standard format, but it was not until 1902 that the divided back came into being, with address and message on one face and a full-size illustration on the other. *Frith & Co* were in the vanguard of postcard development, and Frith's sons Eustace and Cyril continued their father's monumental task, expanding the number of views offered to the public and recording more and more places in Britain, as the coasts and countryside were opened up to mass travel.

Francis Frith died in 1898 at his villa in Cannes, his great project still growing. The archive he created continued in business for another seventy years. By 1970 it contained over a third of a million pictures of 7,000 cities, towns and villages. The massive photographic record Frith has left to us stands as a living monument to a special and very remarkable man.

Frith's Archive: *A Unique Legacy*

FRANCIS FRITH'S legacy to us today is of immense significance and value, for the magnificent archive of evocative photographs he created provides a unique record of change in 7,000 cities, towns and villages throughout Britain over a century and more. Frith and his fellow studio photographers revisited locations many times down the years to update their views, compiling for us an enthralling and colourful pageant of British life and character.

We tend to think of Frith's sepia views of Britain as nostalgic, for most of us use them to conjure up memories of places in our own lives with which we have family associations. It often makes us forget that to Francis Frith they were records of daily life as it was actually being lived in the cities, towns and villages of his day. The Victorian age was one of great and often bewildering change for ordinary people, and though the pictures evoke an impression of slower times, life was as busy and hectic as it is today.

We are fortunate that Frith was a photographer of the people, dedicated to recording the minutiae of everyday life. For it is this sheer wealth of visual data, the painstaking chronicle of changes in dress, transport, street layouts, buildings, housing, engineering and landscape that captivates us so much today. His remarkable images offer us a powerful link with the past and with the lives of our ancestors.

Today's Technology

Computers have now made it possible for Frith's many thousands of images to be accessed almost instantly. In the Frith archive today, each photograph is carefully 'digitised' then stored on a CD Rom. Frith archivists can locate a single photograph amongst thousands within seconds. Views can be catalogued and sorted under a variety of categories of place and content to the immediate benefit of researchers.

Inexpensive reference prints can be created for them at the touch of a mouse button, and a wide range of books and other printed materials assembled and published for a wider, more general readership - in the next twelve months over a hundred Frith local history titles will be published! The day-to-day workings of the archive are very different from how they were in Francis Frith's time: imagine the herculean task of sorting through eleven tons of glass negatives as Frith had to do to locate a particular sequence of pictures!

THE FRANCIS FRITH COLLECTION

Photographic publishers since 1860

HOME | PHOTO SEARCH | BOOKS | PORTFOLIO | GALLERY — MY CART
Products | History | Other Collections | Contact us | Help?

your town,
your village

365,000
photographs of 7,000 towns and villages, taken between 1860 & 1970.

The Frith Archive
The Frith Archive is the remarkable legacy of its energetic and visionary founder. Today, the Frith archive is the only nationally important archive of its kind still in private ownership.

The Collection is world-renowned for the extraordinary quality of its images.

The Gallery
This month The Frith Gallery features images from "Frith's Egypt".

News...
Image update complete.
An additional 5,000 images have been added and the quality of all images has now been improved.

Sample Chapters avaliable.
The first selection of sample chapters from the Frith Book Co.'s extensive range is now available. All are offered in Pdf format for easy downloading and viewing.

explore
FRITH
Search thousands of photographs from one of the worlds' great archives.

Town search
GO

County search
Select a county
GO

the FRITHgallery

See Frith at www. francisfrith.co.uk

Yet the archive still prides itself on maintaining the same high standards of excellence laid down by Francis Frith, including the painstaking cataloguing and indexing of every view.

It is curious to reflect on how the internet now allows researchers in America and elsewhere greater instant access to the archive than Frith himself ever enjoyed. Many thousands of individual views can be called up on screen within seconds on one of the Frith internet sites, enabling people living continents away to revisit the streets of their ancestral home town, or view places in Britain where they have enjoyed holidays. Many overseas researchers welcome the chance to view special theme selections, such as transport, sports, costume and ancient monuments.

We are certain that Francis Frith would have heartily approved of these modern developments in imaging techniques, for he himself was always working at the very limits of Victorian photographic technology.

The Value of the Archive Today

Because of the benefits brought by the computer, Frith's images are increasingly studied by social historians, by researchers into genealogy and ancestory, by architects, town planners, and by teachers and schoolchildren involved in local history projects.

In addition, the archive offers every one of us an opportunity to examine the places where we and our families have lived and worked down the years. Highly successful in Frith's own era, the archive is now, a century and more on, entering a new phase of popularity.

The Past in Tune with the Future

Historians consider the Francis Frith Collection to be of prime national importance. It is the only archive of its kind remaining in private ownership and has been valued at a million pounds. However, this figure is now rapidly increasing as digital technology enables more and more people around the world to enjoy its benefits.

Francis Frith's archive is now housed in an historic timber barn in the beautiful village of Teffont in Wiltshire. Its founder would not recognize the archive office as it is today. In place of the many thousands of dusty boxes containing glass plate negatives and an all-pervading odour of photographic chemicals, there are now ranks of computer screens. He would be amazed to watch his images travelling round the world at unimaginable speeds through network and internet lines.

The archive's future is both bright and exciting. Francis Frith, with his unshakeable belief in making photographs available to the greatest number of people, would undoubtedly approve of what is being done today with his lifetime's work. His photographs, depicting our shared past, are now bringing pleasure and enlightenment to millions around the world a century and more after his death.

Poole & Sandbanks - *An Introduction*

The Borough of Poole includes countryside as well as several communities spreading out from the old Poole town. The borough is a unitary authority with a modern boundary, but it neatly brings back within one council the land between the River Stour and the coast which was the original ancient estate out of which Poole was born. Today over a hundred Canford estate cottages are scattered across the borough, acting as a reminder that Canford in the north-east corner is the 'mother' village. This book covers the wider borough; it also crosses the River Stour to look at Wimborne, from where the Victorian lord of the manor took his title.

The fishing port of Poole was established as an independent town over 750 years ago thanks to the desire of the lord of the manor, William Longespée, Henry II's grandson, to join Louis IX of France in the seventh crusade to the Holy Land. In 1298 William Longespée raised funds by granting a charter to the little port of La Pole in the far south of his estate, five miles from the manor house at Canford Magna on the River Stour. The ship-owners and merchants quickly found 11,200 silver pennies to pay cash in return for the Longespée Charter, which allowed the maritime community to set up a town council and hold a local court. At last the much-disliked ten-mile round trip to refer all matters to the lord of the manor at Canford was unnecessary.

Unfortunately, the deal sent William not just abroad but also to his death during hand-to-hand fighting in Egypt. However, the charter marks the beginning of Poole's expansion into a large borough and the development of the port: today it not only handles cargo and passengers, but even embraces the Royal National Life-boat Institution headquarters.

Today the other Poole borough communities include Parkstone, a Victorian village and grand housing estate; wooded Branksome, which marked the old Dorset county boundary with the 'new' seaside town of Bournemouth; Broadstone, bisected by a Roman road leading to Poole's early quay at Hamworthy, and more recently the home of naturalist Russel Wallace; and Rockley Sands, which was Poole's brave attempt at an early post-war holiday camp, promoted as being in a 'Riviera' setting. This was a repeat of the Victorian marketing of Parkstone as being England's answer to Menton on the French Riviera. Sandbanks, now lined with Britain's most expensive houses, was once a bare sandy spit where Marconi invented radio.

Poole's old town retains its fine setting, with the quay protected from the English Channel by its position inside Europe's largest natural harbour. (In world terms it is exceeded in size only by Sydney Harbour in Australia.) In summer a ferry runs from the quay to the harbour's largest island, Brownsea, where the rare red squirrel survives. In 1907 the Scout movement was born there. Poole Harbour is home to the black-headed gull and the bartailed godwit.

Commercial arrivals passing into the harbour in one typical week can include ships loaded with steel from Rotterdam and Liège and oil from Pembroke. Over the same seven days departures are made for Antwerp, Hamburg, Fowey, Southampton and Teignmouth. Often in sight is the huge 20,000 ton 'Barfleur' which maintains the regular link with Cherbourg. Ships today tend to dock at Hamworthy, but within living memory the old quay was busy with coal being unloaded and steam engines (once led by men carrying red and green flags) pulling trucks along the street. Today passers-by can still watch cockles and scallops being unloaded, although the quay is dominated more by a high Sir Anthony Caro sculpture than tall ships.

A landmark for approaching craft is the tower of the parish church peeping above the low-rise townscape. A church has been on the same site since Longespée's Norman ancestor Patrick d'Evreux built the first in 1142. The present dedication to St James the Great is probably the result of Patrick's pilgrimage to the shrine of St James at Santiago de Compostela in Northern

Spain. Patrick, like William a century later, failed to return from his journey: he was buried in France, having lost a duel. He might have done better to sail direct from Poole to La Coruña and then take the three-day walk south to Santiago. This is how many made the pilgrimage from Poole in the late 14th century, when the boatyard was almost opposite the church's west door.

Today, the church (which was last rebuilt in 1819, and was known to Dorset's author Thomas Hardy) appropriately has choir stalls from the original mother church at Canford Magna. But outside the church there are lamp posts decorated with scallop shells as worn by pilgrims to Santiago. Harry Paye, whose pirate face is painted on the sign at the Old Harry pub in the High Street, was among the local sea-faring residents who took pilgrims to the Galician coast ports.

Poole-born Harry was licensed in 1401 to take up to 80 pilgrims to Spain in his ship the 'Mary'. Unfortunately, he also sometimes sailed across the Bay of Biscay to raid the Spanish coast. He attacked Gijon on the north coast; he also went down to Finisterre in Galicia, which was then literally considered to be 'the end of the earth'. Here he seized the cross from the altar of the little church. Since the object was made of gold, it seems unlikely that he flung it into the sea; but no trace of it has ever been found anywhere in Galicia

or Dorset. To avoid detection Paye sometimes flew a French flag. However, Don Pedro Niño, Count of Belna, knew the identity of the pirate captain, and early one morning in 1406 his Castilian fleet sailed into Poole Harbour. They landed and scaled the church tower whilst a battle raged in the alleys linking the quay with the High Street. With shouts of 'Santiago' and 'Arripay' the invaders killed Paye's brother before being driven away. Harry Paye himself was at sea with his ship on hire to Henry IV.

The typical alleyways - Hosiers, Bull and Buttons Lanes - can be found alongside the waterside Jolly Sailor and Town Arms pubs, which at the start of this century were frequented by smugglers and foreign sailors.

Poole Pottery maintained kilns on the end of the Quay from 1873 until Millennium Year 2000. When tourists were first welcomed in 1919, they were shown round by the 'paintresses', who were developing the ornamental and domestic wares which gave Poole Pottery its reputation and first orders from Liberty's of Regent Street.

Nearby Scaplen's Court houses the earliest carved example of the Poole arms with those scallop shells. The shield dates from the reign of Mary I, who married a Spaniard. However, the Tudors and the Armada threat put an end to the Spanish connection. Poole began to look west to

Newfoundland; this was the source of its 18th-century prosperity, which can be seen in the fine town-houses, Beech Hurst, for example, the Guildhall and even the parish church's pine columns brought on ships' decks.

Poole has recently seen such dramatic change in its industry, housing, port and streetscape that this selection of Frith photographs will bring back memories to many residents and visitors. The town is still changing. Future plans include a dramatic new bridge linking the Poole Pottery site with historic Ballast Quay at Hamworthy. This book should increasingly prove to be both a valuable and an enjoyable record.

Canford

Canford Magna, The Manor 1886 19490
Canford House is Poole's manor house, which dates
from 1450. In the early 19th century this was the
home of William Ponsonby, brother of Byron's lover
Lady Caroline Lamb. Ponsonby's wife, Lady Barbara,
was the sister of the reformer Lord Shaftesbury. In
1846 Sir John Guest, of Guest Keen & Nettlefold,
the iron and steel magnate, bought Canford and
employed Charles Barry, whose Palace of
Westminster was still being built, to enlarge the
house. Guest was so extravagant that he became
known as 'paying Guest'. His son Ivor, who in 1880
was made Lord Wimborne, welcomed many visitors,
including the Prince of Wales (Edward VII), Lady
Wimborne's nephew Winston Churchill, and the
poet Rupert Brooke. The house became Canford
School in 1922.

Canford Magna
The Village 1904 52484
The view is of Magna Road looking north. The village street was then the
main road for travellers to Wimborne from Bournemouth. To the right is a
cottage covered in Virginia creeper which turned scarlet in the autumn.

Canford Magna, The Post Office c1955 C396005
The cottages were built between 1870 and 1872 under the direction of Sir John Guest's wife Charlotte, who was responsible for the many familiar estate cottages now to be found scattered across Poole. The rustic porches were added by her daughter-in-law Cornelia in about 1890.

Canford Magna, The Bridge 1899 43719
The Portland stone bridge, built in 1813, carries the main road from Poole to Wimborne on the far bank of the River Stour. Canford House's western drive runs to the left directly to the bridge, thus avoiding a long road journey.

Wimborne Minster

Wimborne, East Brook 1908 60622
The second bridge before we reach Wimborne town centre is in what is now known as East Street; it spans the River Allen, which joins the River Stour at Canford Bridge. This is the view back towards Canford. The road to the right, by the Wimborne Seed Warehouse, leads to Canford Bridge.

**Wimborne
East Street 1904**
52475
This is the view towards
the town from the River
Allen crossing in East
Street. Looming above
the turning to the right
into the High Street are
the 12th- and 14th-
century towers of
Wimborne Minster,
which made this town a
tourist destination even
in Edward VII's reign.

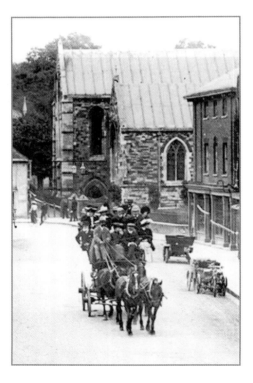

**Wimborne
High Street 1904** 52472
The photographer was looking
down the High Street from an
upper window of the Crown
Hotel in the square. This view,
apart from the traffic, is today
largely unchanged. The tailors on
the right has been rebuilt as a
bank, which has recently
become HSBC.

Wimborne, The Square 1904 52474
This view of the north-east corner of the square shows the Crown Hotel, from where photograph No 52472 was taken on the same day as this view. A century on, the near-empty square has become a busy traffic 'roundabout' with car parking in the middle.

Wimborne, The Square c1965 W105072
Here we see the south side of Wimborne's square at a time when the bank was called the Midland. This, with the nearby Minster, was the heart of the town. Sir John Guest's son Ivor took his title - Lord Wimborne - from the name of the town when he was elevated to the peerage in 1880.

Old Poole

The Guildhall 1898 41165
The Guildhall, forming a climax at the end of Market Street, was built in 1761 with provision for a market on the ground floor. Poole Council continued to meet upstairs until 1931. The Angel to the left remains, but the grocer W Fagg has been replaced by award-winning housing.

◄ **Church Street 1904** 52813
The ancient Guild of St
George almshouses are
pictured in the year they
were restored to provide
accommodation for five
retired people. The house,
first mentioned in 1429,
was originally built for the
four priests serving the four
altars in nearby St James's
church. The building was
extensively altered in 1586
following the loss of the
clergy when Elizabeth I
came to the throne.

The Guildhall 1904
52812
The Guildhall's backdrop has changed today. To the left can be seen the two long windows of the surviving Blue Boar on the corner of Dear Hay Lane, but behind to the right is the Police Station, which was destroyed by fire in the Second World War.

St James's Church 1886 19513
The mediaeval church was replaced by this building in 1819. The first church was a chapel, built here in 1142; at that time a quay to the left brought the water nearer to the churchyard. Today the scene remains largely unchanged.

St James's Church The Interior 1908
61160
The 1820 interior has some features from the earlier building, including central panels on the reredos given in 1736 and the organ, which dates from 1799. The memorial on the far right is to John Masters, merchant of Poole, and dates from 1755.

High Street 1900 46088
W J Bacon, on the corner of the Cornmarket and the High Street, was an ironmongers displaying arms indicating that the Prince of Wales was a customer. Walter Bacon's shop also bore a plaque (now to be seen opposite) recording the meal shared by Charles II and the Duke of Monmouth in a house on the site in 1665. Modern Latimer House has replaced the corner shop.

High Street 1900 46087
Today, a chemist now occupies the left-hand side of the nearest building, whilst the chemist in this picture became Burton's in 1938. It is now the Catalogue Shop. Next door is the Minerva Printing Works; it later became Lookers stationers, bookshop and printers, and is now a mobile 'phone shop.

High Street 1904 52807
The thatched cottage to the left on the
corner of Carter Lane survived until 1919.
It was the home of the Town Crier and bill
poster - a notice in the window reads
'Poole Bill Posting Company'. The cottage
was replaced by Poole's first Woolworth's,
and is now the PamPurred Pets shop.

High Street 1908

61164

This is a similar view to picture No 52807, but taken four years later. The clock on the right, which at this time belonged to watchmaker James Cole, is still a landmark today, but now it advertises the estate agent Tony Newman. The tall building two doors along is now Yates's Wine Lodge.

High Street 1931
84899
We are looking south towards the junction with Carter Lane on the right. Opposite Timothy Whites is the mid 18th-century coaching inn, the London Hotel, now replaced by the Old Harry pub. On the left is Hawkes shoe shop which was established in 1847. Mr Hawke became a pioneer of using the telephone for business.

The Wesleyan ▶ Chapel 1887
19514
This picture, taken from the middle of South Green Road, shows the new Methodist Church in the High Street. It opened in 1880. At the time of the photograph, it still had its railings; today they can only be seen at the side in Chapel Lane.

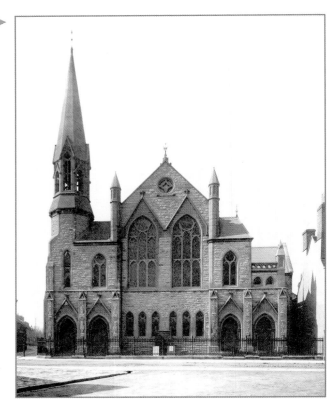

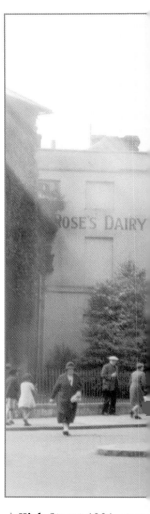

▼ High Street 1904 52808
This is the view south down the High Street from outside Beech Hurst, which is off to the left. The building to the right, next to the Methodist Church and occupied by the undertaker and upholsterer, has now been rebuilt in similar style. It was at this junction that poet Rupert Brooke stopped his horse-drawn caravan in 1910 to make a speech on Poor Law reform.

▲ High Street 1931 84900
We are looking south from outside the Methodist Church on a stretch of the High Street which is now pedestrianised. Kilford's Tea Lounge, on the left beyond Rose's Dairy, is still a café, but it is now called Samritz. The steep gables opposite remain above the new Iceland store.

◀ **High Street
Beech Hurst 1904** 52809
Beech Hurst was built in
1798 for ship's master
Samuel Rolles, who was
involved in Poole's trade
with Newfoundland. The
fine house has been a
school and a furniture shop,
and is now a solicitors'
offices. On the corner next
door is the public library,
which was built in 1889
in part of the garden.

Poole
Quay

The Harbour 1900 46089
This view from Poole Bridge shows the Custom House and the Harbour Office just left of centre. Behind the ship is Yeatman's 18th-century grain warehouse and steam-operated mill. The chimney behind the Harbour Office belonged to Stephen Lewin's Poole Foundry.

Barges and the Quay 1908 61171
The Custom House is facing us - note the railway line points outside. On the left a coal cart awaits its horse outside H & A Burden's, Coal Stores and Ship Chandlers, which owned two small steamships. Two doors away is the Poole Harbour Office.

The Quay 1908 61172
Another view from Poole Bridge shows a barge typical of those which until the 1950s brought clay from the Purbecks for the potteries not only in Poole, but in Seville and Stockholm. Tall ships on the right are moored at Ballast Quay; it was named after the ballast which was loaded prior to sailing for Newfoundland.

The Harbour Office 1904 52815
The Harbour Office dates from 1727; the first floor was extended over the pavement in 1822 to allow for a fire and chimney in the Ballast Master's office above. Next door is Piper & Son, sail makers since 1866, which still occupies the same building. Wedged behind is the part of the Town Cellars which was cut in half by Thames Street.

The Town Cellars 1887 19511
The Town Cellars, with a magnificent timber roof, date from the
13th century, and were the largest of their kind in Europe when
they were built. They were breached in about 1788 when Thames
Street was cut through to the quay. They are now occupied by
Poole Waterfront Museum. Salisbury Street behind has now
become Sarum Street.

◄ **The Harbour c1950**
P72054
The 'Matapan' is moored at the quay to pick up passengers. This is a typical Fifties scene with the then familiar railway trucks and a car. The cyclist would have had to avoid getting his wheels stuck in the railway lines, which ran for over half a mile along West Quay Road to join the main line at Sterte Road.

◄ The Custom House 1904

52814

The Custom House was built in about 1788, a little later than the similar-looking Guildhall. Outside is the Town Beam, which was used for weighing. HM Customs has now relinquished the building, and it has become a wine bar and restaurant. On the quay a steamship is being loaded.

▼ The Harbour c1950

P72060

This is the view from Poole Bridge. The Nissen hut on the left has today given way to a building occupied by the Lifeboat Station and Dorset Police Marine Section. The tall building, now a restaurant, was Yeatman's storehouse, built in about 1790. Hamworthy is on the right bank.

◄ The Harbour c1955

P72160

This unusual view is only normally enjoyed when a tall ship docks. Hamworthy is seen to the left, with Ballast Quay on the extreme left. In the right corner is Poole Pottery; the old Fish Shambles is in the middle of the road in front of the Lord Nelson pub.

The Harbour c1950 P72074

The railway lines, laid along the quay in 1874, became redundant in 1960, and within two years they had disappeared. A cargo often loaded into trucks was coal. A Poole Pottery kiln can be seen in front of the gantry used for unloading coal. To the left is the Portsmouth Hoy pub.

The Bridge 1931 84910

When this photograph was taken from the end of the quay, the bridge linking Poole town and Hamworthy was only four years old. The first bridge on this site was a toll bridge built on massive timber supports in 1835; it was financed by the lord of the manor, William Ponsonby.

Poole Park

The Park 1904 52802
The 26 acres of land for Poole Park was given by lord of the manor Lord Wimborne to mark Victoria's Golden Jubilee in 1887. When it was completed, the Prince of Wales (the future Edward VII) came to stay with Lord Wimborne at Canford Manor in January 1890 before performing the opening ceremony. However, the severe overnight winter weather forced the Prince to formally declare the park open whilst standing in Poole Station.

◄ **The Park Lake 1931**
84902
This scene has changed little since picture No 61176 was taken from the same point over 20 years before. Swans have long been a feature of the park, including appearances, as here in the Thirties and also after the Second World War, of a black swan. The now familiar Canada geese were not introduced until 1957.

The Park Lake 1908

61176

The huge three foot deep salt water lake is part of Poole Harbour's Parkstone Bay; it was enclosed on the south side when the Bournemouth-Poole railway line was built in 1874. Sluice gates in the railway embankment are used to maintain the water level and avoid tidal changes.

The Park and the War Memorial 1931 84904

We see the war memorial just four years after its completion in honour of those from Poole who died in the Great War 1914-1918. Shortly after it was dedicated in 1927, the Prince of Wales (the future Duke of Windsor) came from Bournemouth to lay a wreath in the presence of schoolchildren.

The Park 1931 84903

The shallow lake provided a perfect boating area for many years until recently. Later, the rowing boats were to have competition from pedal craft. Standing out in front of the trees is the new war memorial.

The Small Lake, Poole Park 1908 61177
This is the small fresh water lake created when the road on the right was built across a corner of the park's large sea water lake. Today, the narrow gauge railway runs between the water and the road.

The Miniature Railway, Poole Park c1965 P72164
The popular 10.25 inch narrow gauge railway, laid in 1949, is one the longest established in England. The line runs for half a mile round the smaller lake. Steam was replaced by diesel in 1970, but the four carriages are from the original train.

Parkstone Road

Parkstone Road 1898 41171
Here Parkstone Road runs gently downhill to Poole town. On the
right is Haydon Cottage, which today is a therapy clinic. The
house to the left is, in the 21st century, not a residence either
but is occupied by the accountants Wheatley Pearce.

◀ **Parkstone
The Church 1904**
52795
The east end of St Peter's church is seen from Church Road. St Peter's dates from 1833. It was the scene of Robert Baden-Powell's wedding in 1912; his bride was Olave Soames from nearby Lilliput overlooking Poole Harbour.

Parkstone

◄ **Parkstone, The Park 1898** 41176
Parkstone Park, which opened in 1888, was originally Three Acre Field. It was bought by the council from Lord Wimborne for £560 and turned into a garden to mark Queen Victoria's Jubilee, which had been celebrated the previous year. A stream which ran through the middle is now culverted. The end shop is a chemist's, J A Haynes, which soon moved a few doors to the left. Although now a restaurant, the words 'Mentone Pharmacy' in brass have been retained. At the time this picture was taken, Parkstone was being compared to Menton in the south of France; there is also a Mentone Road.

◄ **Parkstone Bank Corner 1904**
52788
The bank was built in 1894 as the Wilts & Dorset Bank on the main road to Bournemouth at the Church Road cross-roads at the bottom of Castle Hill. Today it is Lloyds TSB. Parkstone Park is to the left.

▼ Parkstone, Castle Hill 1900 46095

The main road from Poole to Bournemouth was called Parkstone Hill until the 1890s, when a castellated house called The Castle was built on high ground near the top. The site is now the south end of Glen Road.

▼ Parkstone, Sandecotes 1900 46098

The two boys are posing at the south end of Highbridge Road near the junction with Belle Vue Road. The house opposite is Broomrigg; like the one to the left, it has today been demolished to make way for modern flats.

▲ Parkstone, Sandecotes 1904 52785

Alton Road is in the foreground. The house on the right is Kenwood, which has its entrance in Corfe View Road. Immediately behind is Eaton Hall in Highmoor Road. The new house to the right is 8 Corfe View Road, which retains its stained glass in the stairway window.

◄ **Parkstone**
From the Pier 1900 46099
The pier is at the bottom
of Evening Hill. The hut has
today been superseded by
a larger building for the East
Dorset Sailing Club. Both
houses in this photograph
survive. On the left is Shore
Lodge, and on the right is
Evening Hill Grange.

Parkstone
Shore Road 1904 52786
Here we see Shore Road, between Haven Road and Brudenell
Avenue, in the days before heavy traffic. The embankment wall
with lamp posts was built in 1894. Now the busy road has required
the bank in the picture to be removed. In the centre is Evening Hill
Grange near Parkstone Pier.

Brownsea Island

Brownsea Island
From Sandbanks 1898 41188

The 500-acre Brownsea Island, the largest of Poole Harbour's islands, was in the care of monks from Cerne Abbas until their monastery was dissolved in 1539 by Henry VIII. He built the Castle in 1547, although the present familiar outline dates from the 1850s. In 1907 Robert Baden-Powell held the first Scout camp on the South Shore. However, from 1927 until 1961 the Castle was occupied by banker's daughter Mary Bonham Christie. She lived as a recluse, allowing nature to take over the island, which was closed to visitors. Brownsea Island is now in the care of the National Trust, whilst the Castle has become a John Lewis Partnership holiday home.

◄ **Brownsea Island The Castle 1891** 29623
We see Brownsea Castle from the south-west, with Canford Cliffs' high ground visible across the harbour to the right. The building was originally part of a string of coastal defences built by Henry VIII from Portland to Southsea. An early owner was Elizabeth I's Lord Chancellor Christopher Hatton.

Brownsea Island
The Castle 1891 29621
This is the view from the quay where visitors land today. Ahead is the glass-roofed approach to the castle from the castle's own landing stage by the twin towers. The house on the right, now the café, was built in 1842 for the Chief Coastguard Officer and his family.

Brownsea Island
The Villa 1891 29625
The Villa was built in the 1850s as the vicarage for the newly-built church. But from 1870 until 1891 the house was the home of island owner George Cavendish-Bentinck, who preferred to live there rather than the Castle. The Villa is now within the nature reserve, which embraces a heronry.

Brownsea Island
The Castle 1891 29624
A view of the Castle taken in the year Brownsea's owner George Cavendish-Bentinck died. He had bought the island in 1870, but by 1887 he had to admit that he could not make the pottery on the far side pay. He chose to live in The Villa, which can be seen in the background, and gave the Castle to his son Frederick as a wedding present.

**Brownsea Island
The Castle 1904** 52801
The 'Elettra', Marconi's
yellow-funnelled steam
yacht, is moored in front
of Brownsea Castle. At
this time the island was
owned by Charles Van
Raalte, who the previous
year had changed the
name of the island from
Branksea to Brownsea
to avoid confusion with
Branksome on the
mainland.

**Brownsea Island
The Castle 1898**
41187
The view is from the sand dunes on the Sandbanks peninsula. During this time the Castle was being restored following a fire in 1898. By 1901 the interior was almost complete, and the owner Major Kenneth Balfour MP put the island on the market.

◀ **Sandbanks**
The Haven Hotel 1900
46102
The coastguard lookout is where the ferry now docks. At the turn of the century the ferry was only for foot passengers. To the right is the Haven Hotel, and one of Guglielmo Marconi's radio masts. Four years earlier he had sent the first wireless message from here; he was still a regular visitor in 1900.

Sandbanks

◀ **Studland, The Ferry c1955** S226027
The view is of Sandbanks Ferry from Shell Bay looking towards Poole's sandy peninsula. The chain ferry began in 1926, saving 15 miles on the journey to Swanage. This is the new diesel vessel which had just replaced steam; it has now been superseded by a larger 'floating bridge'.

◀ **Sandbanks Poole Head 1904**
52797
The photographer is looking east towards Poole Head, at the end of the long high cliff of Poole Bay which includes Bournemouth. To the left, Banks Road runs alongside Poole Harbour. The huts have now been replaced by some of the world's most expensive houses.

Sandbanks, Shore Road 1912 66148
New houses on the Sandbanks peninsula can be seen in this photograph taken from Shore Road inside Poole Harbour. There is clay under the sand, which enabled more houses to be erected following the opening of the Haven Hotel in 1898. Soon after that, tobacco baron Sir Ernest Wills built himself a holiday home.

Sandbanks and Brownsea Island 1900 46101
Some of the buildings on the tip of Sandbanks are coastguard cottages. Charles Van Raalte, who bought Brownsea Island in 1901, purchased some adjoining sandy land so as to be qualified to accept an invitation from Poole Corporation for him to be Mayor.

Branksome

Westbourne
County Gates 1913 66144
This gateway was called Packe Gates when it was the entrance to the long drive to clifftop
Branksome Tower, built for Sir Charles Packe in 1852. The lodge became known as
County Gates because this junction on the main Bournemouth-Poole road was also the
boundary between both the two towns and Hampshire and Dorset. The building was
demolished in 1975, but the pedestrian archway can now be found in Branksome Chine
(just south of Wilderton Road). The Avenue was the main drive to the now demolished
Branksome Tower, which in 1890 became a popular hotel. Poole's tram line was laid as
far as County Gates in 1901; it joined to Bournemouth's existing network four years later.

Branksome Chine 1890 25519
This wooded valley was known to young Winston Churchill when he stayed with his aunt Lady
Wimborne at her nearby holiday house. Three years after the picture was taken, 18-year-old
Winston injured himself whilst trying to slide down a pine tree in the next door Branksome
Dene Chine. It was during his convalescence that he resolved to enter Parliament.

Alum Chine

Westbourne, Alum Chine 1918 68071
Alum Chine, just over the boundary in Bournemouth, is named after
a short-lived alum works opened in 1564 by Poole's lord of the
manor, Lord Mountjoy of Canford. Ahead can be seen Canford Cliffs
and the land dropping down to Sandbanks. Poole Bay is to the left.

◀ **Broadstone
The Golf Course
c1960** B735030
Broadstone Golf Club
was laid out in 1897 by
Lord Wimborne for
private use by his family
and friends. The 18-hole
course was opened in
1898 by the future
Prime Minister A J
Balfour. It is now
considered to be one of
the best heathland
courses in the south of
England.

Broadstone

◄ **Broadstone, The Broadway c1960** B735023
Broadstone is named after Broadstone Farm, which in turn took its name from broad stones spanning a stream. One is outside the Stepping Stones pub. The main road, which includes The Broadway, which we see here, was built in 1765. Baxter's is now Bath Travel. The railway bridge is at the far end. The now-closed railway arrived in 1847, but since there were few houses, a station was not built until 1872. There were just five villas here in 1888 when Lord Wimborne built the school. An early resident was the naturalist Alfred Russel Wallace, a contemporary of Charles Darwin, who lived at the now demolished Old Orchard in Wallace Road from 1889 until his death in 1913.

◄ **Broadstone Dunyeats Road c1955**
B735013
The parade of shops remains, but with 21st-century changes. Today the chimney has gone, and the windows have recently been replaced. The telephone box in front of the newsagents has moved across the road to behind the camera. The old school sign in the centre of the photograph warns motorists that the village school is on the left.

Longfleet Road

Longfleet Road 1904 52811
The foreground of this view is now Falkland Square and the Dolphin Centre. C T Snook, on the right, is also the Post Office; it was the predecessor of the Dolphin Centre's Longfleet Post Office, which is almost on the same site. In front of the trees on the left is a toll house. Today this spot is the centre of the roundabout north of the shopping centre. Behind the trees is the spire of St Mary's church in Longfleet.

Longfleet Road 1908
61167
This is a similar view to No 52811 taken four years earlier. The Holmes Refreshment Rooms was part of the Temperance Hotel, which later became the Dolphin Hotel. Slightly more visible is the toll house at the beginning of Wimborne Road to the left. Newspapers were sold there on Sundays when the newsagents were closed.

◀ **Longfleet Church 1887** 19519
We see the new St Mary's church from the north side of Longfleet Road, which is now very busy. To the right is the entrance to Parish Road, which is named after a former vicar. Today the gate has disappeared and the trees have grown.

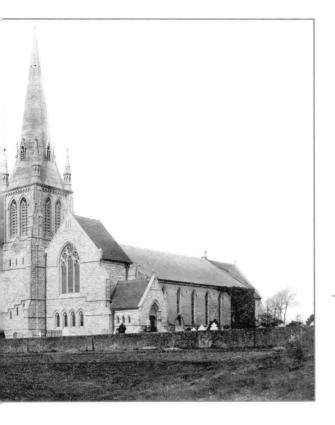

Longfleet

◀ **Longfleet Church and Schools 1887** 19520
St Mary's was built in 1833 by lord of the manor
William Ponsonby. He was a Liberal Party supporter,
and not popular with Conservative supporters; they
built nearby St Peter's in Parkstone, which was
consecrated the day after St Mary's. This view is
taken from the allotments, now occupied by Poole's
modern hospital. Today a south transept has been
added.

◀ **People's Park 1898**
41166
St Mary's church at
Longfleet is seen from
the lake in the new
Poole Park. The 108ft-
high spire means that
the church remains a
landmark, although
today it is surrounded
by buildings. The
houses indicate the
line of Parkstone Road.

Constitution Hill

◀ **Parkstone, From Constitution Hill 1904** 52782
The view from Constitution Hill across Poole and its
harbour remains a tourist attraction today. We can see a
tram climbing North Road. When the trams first ran in
1901, only one had brakes strong enough to use the hill,
so passengers had to change at the top.

◀ **From Constitution
Hill 1908** 61157
This view from the hill
top on to North Road is
now blocked by trees
planted to prevent
erosion. The tram is at
the junction of Cotes
Avenue. All the large
Victorian houses have
gone, except for the one
on the left. Parkstone's
St Peter's Church can be
seen behind.

Poole Grammar School

Poole Secondary School 1908 61173
The year 1907 is carved in the stone, but this picture was taken the following year when the school
opened for 200 secondary age boys and girls. In 1927 the school became the Grammar School,
and a decade later it became a boys only school, with girls diverted to Parkstone Grammar School.
Poole Grammar School vacated the building, which had a quadrangle at the rear, for new buildings
on Gravel Hill which were opened by Princess Margaret in 1966. The old building briefly became
Seldown School before being demolished to make way for the Seldown Bridge, carrying traffic past
the Dolphin Swimming Pool. The school was adjacent to Ladies' Walking Field on the site of the
rope works, where women walking the ropes had been a common sight.

Rockley Sands

Rockley Sands
The Path to the Orchard c1960 P72134
This is Turling Farm on Ham Common, overlooking Lytchett
Bay in Poole Harbour. This area is now part of Rockley Park,
which was at first marketed as Poole's 'Riviera'. The land
beyond the railway running below has now become Turlin
Moor housing estate. Today the farm building has gone; the
site, now covered by caravans, is known as Orchard Bank.

◄ **Rockley Sands
The Super-Market
c1960** P72188
Well-filled shelves in the camp shop provide daily basics for self-catering families. Supermarkets were still a modern idea. Unlike today, there is a large amount of tinned food and soup available, as most accommodation did not have a fridge.

◀ **Rockley Sands
The Super-Market
c1960** P72187
Rockley Sands was one
of the earliest holiday
camps. It catered for
family groups who
wanted outdoor holidays
with plenty of activities.
For years this was Poole
Council's only
concession to the
tourism industry, which
did well in neighbouring
Bournemouth.

▼ **Rockley Sands
The Palladium c1965**
P72307
The Palladium Bar was
opened when the site
was first developed for
leisure. The zig-zag roof
now covers a swimming
pool, and the displaced
bar is in a new part of
the extended building. To
the right behind the car
is the Miniature Zoo. Just
behind the roof is
wooded Beacon Hill.

◀ **Rockley Sands
The Beach c1960**
P72130
This is the most well-
known part of Rockley
Sands, as it is seen from
the Weymouth to
Waterloo trains running
along the embankment
built across the harbour.
On the left is a water
tower serving steam
engines. The main camp
road ran directly on to
this beach.

▼ **Rockley Sands, The Sands c1960** P72127

Rockley Point has now developed into a sailing school and boatyard. Also new today are the substantial caravans now dotted under the trees on the viewpoint. The dark Arne peninsula can be seen against the line of the chalk ridge of the Purbeck Hills.

▼ **Rockley Sands, Water Skiing c1960** P72243

Water-skiing was just one of the many new sports offered to guests at Rockley Sands. Behind is Bay Hollow: there are now some trees on the cliff, and the path to the right has become steps. Today there are still as many as 17 caravans in the prime position.

▲ **Rockley Sands The Beach c1960**

P72221

This beach in tidal Poole Harbour was handy for campers here in the northern part of Poole, who were some distance from the extensive beaches at Sandbanks and Canford Cliffs. The beach furniture and donkeys have long disappeared from the summer scene at Rockley Sands.

**Rockley Sands
The Boating Centre
c1960** P72131
Here we see the inlet at Rockley Point before its east end was dammed to became a safe boating lake for pedaloes. The chimneys of the Junction Hotel can be seen behind the railway embankment. The lonely railway building has now gone.

▼ **Rockley Sands, Bay Hollow c1965** P72356
In the Sixties 100,000 visitors a year were holidaying at Rockley Sands Caravan Park; it covered some 600 acres of harbourside heathland and pine wood. These caravans are on the west side of the wood just above Rockley Point.

▼ **Rockley Sands, Rockley Point c1965** P72264
This is the view south along the beach from Rockley Point. The road to the main buildings and Poole can be seen running up from the beach by the ice cream hut. Today both the ice cream hut and the gorse on the beach have disappeared.

▲ **Rockley Sands Bay Hollow c1965**
P72257
The scene to the north-west from the view point. Rockley Jetty Point, with its rail link, is across the water, with Holton Heath and Wareham Forest in the distance. In the foreground is the remains of Ham Common, which today is a nature reserve.

Rockley Sands
The Miniature Railway
c1965 P72289
Rockley Sands attempted to
run a railway to rival the
popular steam railway at
Poole Park. However, the
diesel Atlantic Coast Line
proved less successful than
the old-fashioned steam
railway. Other attractions
included a games room, an
amusement centre and a
'television theatre'.

Rockley Sands, Sunset over Bay Hollow c1960 P72122
The caravans overlook Poole Harbour and Holton Heath. Across the water on the left is Rockley Jetty, used for unloading cordite. A short railway line, complete with a turntable, ran from the pier, allowing trains to take the cargo to the armaments factory near Holton Heath Station.

Rockley Sands, Sunset c1965 P72145
Campers drift back to their caravans after watching one of Poole Harbour's famous sunsets. At this time, the overnight accommodation included access to 'modern hygienic washrooms fitted with hot and cold showers, wash-basins and main sanitation'.

Index

The Francis Frith Collection Titles

www.francisfrith.co.uk

The Francis Frith Collection publishes over 100 new titles each year. A selection of those currently available is listed below. For latest catalogue please contact The Francis Frith Collection. **Town Books** 96 pages, approximately 75 photos. **County and Themed Books** 128 pages, approximately 135 photos (unless specified). All titles hardback with laminated case and jacket, except those indicated pb (paperback)

Accrington Old and New
Alderley Edge and Wilmslow
Amersham, Chesham and Rickmansworth
Andover
Around Abergavenny
Around Alton
Aylesbury
Barnstaple
Bedford
Bedfordshire
Berkshire Living Memories
Berkshire PA
Blackpool Pocket Album
Bognor Regis
Bournemouth
Bradford
Bridgend
Bridport
Brighton and Hove
Bristol
Buckinghamshire
Calne Living Memories
Camberley PA
Canterbury Cathedral
Cardiff Old and New
Chatham and the Medway Towns
Chelmsford
Chepstow Then and Now
Cheshire
Cheshire Living Memories
Chester
Chesterfield
Chigwell
Christchurch
Churches of East Cornwall
Clevedon
Clitheroe
Corby Living Memories
Cornish Coast
Cornwall Living Memories
Cotswold Living Memories
Cotswold Pocket Album
Coulsdon, Chipstead and Woodmanstern
County Durham
Cromer, Sheringham and Holt
Dartmoor Pocket Album
Derby
Derbyshire
Derbyshire Living Memories
Devon
Devon Churches
Dorchester

Dorset Coast PA
Dorset Living Memories
Dorset Villages
Down the Dart
Down the Severn
Down the Thames
Dunmow, Thaxted and Finchingfield
Durham
East Anglia PA
East Devon
East Grinstead
Edinburgh
Ely and The Fens
Essex PA
Essex Second Selection
Essex: The London Boroughs
Exeter
Exmoor
Falmouth
Farnborough, Fleet and Aldershot
Folkestone
Frome
Furness and Cartmel Peninsulas
Glamorgan
Glasgow
Glastonbury
Gloucester
Gloucestershire
Greater Manchester
Guildford
Hailsham
Hampshire
Harrogate
Hastings and Bexhill
Haywards Heath Living Memories
Heads of the Valleys
Heart of Lancashire PA
Helston
Herefordshire
Horsham
Humberside PA
Huntingdon, St Neots and St Ives
Hythe, Romney Marsh and Ashford
Ilfracombe
Ipswich PA
Isle of Wight
Isle of Wight Living Memories
King's Lynn
Kingston upon Thames
Lake District PA
Lancashire Living Memories
Lancashire Villages

Available from your local bookshop or from the publisher

The Francis Frith Collection Titles (continued)

Lancaster, Morecombe and Heysham Pocket Album
Leeds PA
Leicester
Leicestershire
Lincolnshire Living Memoires
Lincolnshire Pocket Album
Liverpool and Merseyside
London PA
Ludlow
Maidenhead
Maidstone
Malmesbury
Manchester PA
Marlborough
Matlock
Merseyside Living Memories
Nantwich and Crewe
New Forest
Newbury Living Memories
Newquay to St Ives
North Devon Living Memories
North London
North Wales
North Yorkshire
Northamptonshire
Northumberland
Northwich
Nottingham
Nottinghamshire PA
Oakham
Odiham Then and Now
Oxford Pocket Album
Oxfordshire
Padstow
Pembrokeshire
Penzance
Petersfield Then and Now
Plymouth
Poole and Sandbanks
Preston PA
Ramsgate Old and New
Reading Pocket Album
Redditch Living Memories
Redhill to Reigate
Rhondda Valley Living Mems
Richmond
Ringwood
Rochdale
Romford PA
Salisbury PA
Scotland
Scottish Castles
Sevenoaks and Tonbridge
Sheffield and South Yorkshire PA
Shropshire
Somerset
South Devon Coast
South Devon Living Memories
South East London
Southampton PA
Southend PA

Southport
Southwold to Aldeburgh
Stourbridge Living Memories
Stratford upon Avon
Stroud
Suffolk
Suffolk PA
Surrey Living Memories
Sussex
Sutton
Swanage and Purbeck
Swansea Pocket Album
Swindon Living Memories
Taunton
Teignmouth
Tenby and Saundersfoot
Tiverton
Torbay
Truro
Uppingham
Villages of Kent
Villages of Surrey
Villages of Sussex PA
Wakefield and the Five Towns Living Memories
Warrington
Warwick
Warwickshire PA
Wellingborough Living Memories
Wells
Welsh Castles
West Midlands PA
West Wiltshire Towns
West Yorkshire
Weston-super-Mare
Weymouth
Widnes and Runcorn
Wiltshire Churches
Wiltshire Living memories
Wiltshire PA
Wimborne
Winchester PA
Windermere
Windsor
Wirral
Wokingham and Bracknell
Woodbridge
Worcester
Worcestershire
Worcestershire Living Memories
Wyre Forest
York PA
Yorkshire
Yorkshire Coastal Memories
Yorkshire Dales
Yorkshire Revisited

See Frith books on the internet at www.francisfrith.co.uk

FRITH PRODUCTS & SERVICES

Francis Frith would doubtless be pleased to know that the pioneering publishing venture he started in 1860 still continues today. Over a hundred and forty years later, The Francis Frith Collection continues in the same innovative tradition and is now one of the foremost publishers of vintage photographs in the world. Some of the current activities include:

Interior Decoration

Today Frith's photographs can be seen framed and as giant wall murals in thousands of pubs, restaurants, hotels, banks, retail stores and other public buildings throughout the country. In every case they enhance the unique local atmosphere of the places they depict and provide reminders of gentler days in an increasingly busy and frenetic world.

Product Promotions

Frith products are used by many major companies to promote the sales of their own products or to reinforce their own history and heritage. Frith promotions have been used by Hovis bread, Courage beers, Scots Porage Oats, Colman's mustard, Cadbury's foods, Mellow Birds coffee, Dunhill pipe tobacco, Guinness, and Bulmer's Cider.

Genealogy and Family History

As the interest in family history and roots grows world-wide, more and more people are turning to Frith's photographs of Great Britain for images of the towns, villages and streets where their ancestors lived; and, of course, photographs of the churches and chapels where their ancestors were christened, married and buried are an essential part of every genealogy tree and family album.

Frith Products

All Frith photographs are available Framed or just as Mounted Prints and Posters (size 23 x 16 inches). These may be ordered from the address below. From time to time other products - Address Books, Maps, etc - are available.

The Internet

Already ninety thousand Frith photographs can be viewed and purchased on the internet through the Frith websites and a myriad of partner sites.

For more detailed information on Frith companies and products, look at these sites:

www.francisfrith.co.uk
www.francisfrith.com
(for North American visitors)

See the complete list of Frith Books at:

www.francisfrith.co.uk

This web site is regularly updated with the latest list of publications from The Francis Frith Collection. If you wish to buy books relating to another part of the country that your local bookshop does not stock, you may purchase on-line.

For further information, trade, or author enquiries please contact us at the address below:
The Francis Frith Collection, Frith's Barn, Teffont, Salisbury, Wiltshire, England SP3 5QP.
Tel: +44 (0)1722 716 376 Fax: +44 (0)1722 716 881 Email: sales@francisfrith.co.uk

See Frith books on the internet at www.francisfrith.co.uk

FREE PRINT OF YOUR CHOICE

Mounted Print
Overall size 14 x 11 inches (355 x 280mm)

Choose any Frith photograph in this book.
Simply complete the Voucher opposite and
return it with your remittance for £3.50 (to cover
postage and handling) and we will print the
photograph of your choice in SEPIA (size 11 x 8
inches) and supply it in a cream mount with a
burgundy rule line (overall size 14 x 11 inches).
Please note: aerial photographs and
photographs with a reference number
starting with a "Z" are not Frith photographs
and cannot be supplied under this offer.
Offer valid for delivery to one UK address only.

PLUS: **Order additional Mounted Prints
at HALF PRICE - £9.50 each** (normally £19.00)
If you would like to order more Frith prints from
this book, possibly as gifts for friends and family,
you can buy them at half price (with no
additional postage and handling costs).

PLUS: **Have your Mounted Prints framed**
For an extra £18.00 per print you can have your
mounted print(s) framed in an elegant polished
wood and gilt moulding, overall size
16 x 13 inches (no additional postage and
handling required).

IMPORTANT!

**These special prices are only available if you use
this form to order. You must use the ORIGINAL
VOUCHER on this page (no copies permitted). We
can only despatch to one UK address. This offer
cannot be combined with any other offer.**

Send completed Voucher form to:
**The Francis Frith Collection, Frith's Barn,
Teffont, Salisbury, Wiltshire SP3 5QP**

CHOOSE A PHOTOGRAPH FROM THIS BOOK

Voucher for **FREE** and Reduced Price Frith Prints

*Please do not photocopy this voucher. Only the original is valid,
so please fill it in, cut it out and return it to us with your order.*

Picture ref no	Page no	Qty	Mounted @ £9.50	Framed + £18.00	Total Cost £
		1	Free of charge*	£	£
			£9.50	£	£
			£9.50	£	£
			£9.50	£	£
			£9.50	£	£
			£9.50	£	£

*Please allow 28 days
for delivery.
Offer available to one
UK address only*

* Post & handling	£3.50
Total Order Cost	£

Title of this book . . . .

I enclose a cheque/postal order for £ . . . .
made payable to 'The Francis Frith Collection'

OR please debit my Mastercard / Visa / Maestro card,
details below

Card Number

Issue No (Maestro only)   Valid from (Maestro)

Expires   Signature

Name Mr/Mrs/Ms ....

Address ....

....

....

.... Postcode ....

Daytime Tel No ....

Email ....

Valid to 31/12/12

Would you like to find out more about Francis Frith?

We have recently recruited some entertaining speakers who are happy to visit local groups, clubs and societies to give an illustrated talk documenting Frith's travels and photographs. If you are a member of such a group and are interested in hosting a presentation, we would love to hear from you.

Our speakers bring with them a small selection of our local town and county books, together with sample prints. They are happy to take orders. A small proportion of the order value is donated to the group who have hosted the presentation. The talks are therefore an excellent way of fundraising for small groups and societies.

Can you help us with information about any of the Frith photographs in this book?

We are gradually compiling an historical record for each of the photographs in the Frith archive. It is always fascinating to find out the names of the people shown in the pictures, as well as insights into the shops, buildings and other features depicted.

If you recognize anyone in the photographs in this book, or if you have information not already included in the author's caption, do let us know. We would love to hear from you, and will try to publish it in future books or articles.

Our production team

Frith books are produced by a small dedicated team at offices in the converted Grade II listed 18th-century barn at Teffont near Salisbury, illustrated above. Most have worked with the Frith Collection for many years. All have in common one quality: they have a passion for the Frith Collection. The team is constantly expanding, but currently includes:

Paul Baron, Phillip Brennan, Jason Buck, John Buck, Ruth Butler, Heather Crisp, David Davies, Louis du Mont, Isobel Hall, Lucy Hart, Julian Hight, Peter Horne, James Kinnear, Karen Kinnear, Tina Leary, Stuart Login, David Marsh, Sue Molloy, Glenda Morgan, Wayne Morgan, Sarah Roberts, Kate Rotondetto, Dean Scource, Eliza Sackett, Terence Sackett, Sandra Sampson, Adrian Sanders, Sandra Sanger, Julia Skinner, Miles Smith, Lewis Taylor, Shelley Tolcher, Lorraine Tuck, David Turner, Amanita Wainwright and Ricky Williams.